# Growi… es in Small Groups

## A Resource for Leaders

**Anna Creedon**
Assistant Curate

**Sally Dakin**
Retired Priest

**GROVE BOOKS LIMITED**
**RIDLEY HALL RD CAMBRIDGE CB3 9HU**

# Contents





**First Impression** April 2023
**ISSN** 2753-9369
**ISBN** 978 1 78827 311 4

# 1 Introduction

The aim of this booklet is to enable small group leaders to think through the significance of purpose, leadership, context and materials for their group. We hope those involved in this important ministry will be able to reflect on how their group might more effectively equip its members for everyday discipleship. In other words, how might your group support and encourage people in their discipleship as they seek to live more 'Jesus-shaped lives'?

One of our key themes is the balance between *comfort* and *challenge*, as we believe that getting this balance right can make a big difference. Ideally issues such as this would be addressed when a group is first launched, but it is never too late to reset its course.

The booklet has been co-authored by Anna Creedon and Sally Dakin, with both of us contributing to each chapter. Anna's interest in small groups grew during her time as a secondary school teacher; then, as she trained for ordained ministry, she did her doctoral research on the transformative potential of engaging with the Bible in small groups, which has since been published.[1]

Sally has extensive experience in leading small groups across a variety of settings, both in the workplace (including the NHS) and in the church, in the UK and abroad, and has also been involved in leading various groups online.

Our aim is to offer practical help to group leaders, rather than arguing the case for small groups—this is tackled by Laurence Singlehurst and Trevor Withers in their recent booklet, *Making Missional Disciples through Small Groups: Why Small Groups Are Essential for Today,* which we highly recommend.[2]

We hope that whether you have been leading a small group for many years or have just taken responsibility for launching or leading one, you will find that this booklet helps you to reflect on how your role as leader might contribute to the effectiveness of your group. If your group is struggling, we trust that you too will find helpful material here.

# 2 What is the Purpose of Your Small Group?

Here we consider the importance of purpose in small groups.

> If you are currently part of a small group, you might find it helpful to take a few moments now to consider what you see as the purpose of the group.

## Why is Purpose Important in a Small Group?

Ultimately, *having a purpose gives a small group a reason for existing*. However, there are many groups without an explicit purpose, because they have evolved naturally. Douglas differentiates between 'natural' and 'created' groups, and suggests that one of the key differences between these two types of group is a sense of purpose.[3] Examples of naturally occurring groups include family units and friendship groups. By contrast, so-called 'artificial' groups are usually created with a particular purpose in mind, for example, running clubs, art groups or choirs. This sense of purpose brings together people who may never have met otherwise, and who may have no other reason to belong together.

So when it comes to creating a small group, having a clear purpose helps to bring people together around a common interest, vision or objective, and having a clear sense of this purpose will make it much easier to achieve.

## Common Purposes

Small groups exist for a whole variety of purposes, some more obvious than others. So the purpose of a *prayer* group is presumably to pray, and a *Bible study* group probably has studying the Bible as its main purpose. However, groups often change and evolve over time; there might be changes in membership, in practices, in focus etc…and this will affect the purpose of the group. And it is important to note that many groups will never have defined their purpose explicitly; there may be an assumed purpose that is shared by members of the group, but it has never been openly stated, discussed or agreed upon.

As part of Anna's research, she asked participants, 'What do you believe to be the primary purpose of a church-related small group?' A range of answers was offered, which broadly speaking related to two main themes: *relating to others* and *maturing in faith*. Responses focused on relating to others used words like 'fellowship,' 'supporting' and 'sharing,' while 'grow' and 'build' were used by those emphasizing the importance of maturing in faith.[4] These were not seen as mutually exclusive: one group member defined the purpose of a small group as 'fellowship and spiritual growth.'[5] Groups can certainly have more than one purpose, and together they can enhance the group's effectiveness.

Of course, members of the same group may have different ideas about what the purpose of their group is or should be. Therefore it can be helpful to ask them periodically what they see as the purpose of the group, and whether they feel the group is fulfilling this purpose.

## Developing and Defining a Clear Purpose

You may be leading a small group that has been running for a significant period of time or you might be starting a new group—or you may be somewhere in between. Clearly, this will have a bearing on how you might go about developing and defining a purpose for your group, so you will probably find one of the sections below more helpful than the other, depending on your situation.

### New Small Groups

If you have just become the leader of a new group, then you have a great opportunity to establish the group's purpose right from the start. If your church sets out clear guidance about what such groups are for, you will need to bear this in mind as you develop the purpose of your particular group.

If your group has just started, then it might be helpful to use one of your first few sessions to discuss what the group members see as the purpose of the group. These questions may be useful:

- Why did you join the group?
- What are you hoping to get out of the group?
- What do you imagine doing together when we meet? (such as socializing, eating together, worshipping, praying, Bible study, community projects)
- What would you like to see as the main purpose of the group?

Person-centred questions like these can help to clarify what people see as the purpose of the group—a bottom-up approach. This kind of discussion early on can also reveal wildly different ideas about what the group is for, which can then be explored. Once you have reached the stage of identifying the purpose, or purposes, of the group, then you could write this down to formalize it.

## Existing Small Groups

If you have been leading a small group or recently taken on the leadership of a group that has been running for some time, it can seem rather more daunting to ask what the purpose of the group is. What if no-one is really sure? What if people disagree, potentially causing a split in the group? However, taking the opportunity to stop and reflect on the history of the group, and how it has evolved over time, can be a really helpful exercise, and may also help to establish what direction the group is taking.

The following questions could form the basis of a discussion about the purpose of an existing group:

- Why did you originally join the group?
- What made you stay?
- How do you feel you have benefited from being part of the group?
- What would you like the group to focus on going forwards?

Whether you are leading a new or existing small group, it is important to ask not only what are *your* purposes for the group, but also what are *God's* purposes? Might it be that God gifts the church with groups in order to grow disciples, living Jesus-shaped lives in all our roles and relationships, local or global? Walter Wink certainly sees this transformational approach as the ideal purpose of small groups:

> If in this approach, we make our conscious goal the transformation of persons toward the divine possibilities inherent in them, then we cannot be content with simply 'having a good group,' or helping people to 'understand the Bible better,' or 'giving them more information,' or even 'trying to build fellowship.' These are temptations to do the good, not the better. If nothing less than human transformation is our goal, then everything we do must be aimed at enabling people to become more precisely and fully the selves that they need to be in order to be available to God as effective agents of the kingdom.[6]

In her research, Anna focused specifically on this purpose—and on the role of biblical engagement in bringing it about.

It would be helpful to spend some time in prayer, not only as you meet together in the group, but also as individuals alone with God, deliberately waiting on God and seeking to discern his purposes. You might reflect on some Bible passages together, especially ones that members of the group have felt led to or feel are relevant. These verses may also be useful:

> 'Do not conform to the pattern of this world, but be transformed by the renewing of your mind.' (Rom 12.2a)
>
> 'And let us consider how we may spur one another on toward love and good deeds, not giving up meeting together, as some are in the habit of doing, but encouraging one another.' (Heb 10.24–25a)
>
> 'They devoted themselves to the apostles' teaching and to fellowship, to the breaking of bread and to prayer...' (Acts 2.42–47)

We would encourage all small groups to regularly reflect upon how God might be seeking to use the group to bring about his purposes.

## Yes, but...

Perhaps in an ideal world all our groups would be clear about their purpose(s), and each meeting would represent another step along their journey to fulfilment. But besides purpose there are two other important ingredients: issues relating to the group as a whole, and issues relating to the individual members.[7]

The key *group* issues which determine its ultimate effectiveness are the quality of the relationships group members have with each other, and their willingness to commit themselves to working together towards the achievement of the group's purpose. These issues are connected with the needs of the *individuals* in the group, which might be summarized, in the language of Transactional Analysis, as *structure, strokes* and *stimulation*.[8] *Structure* represents the basic human need for order and control; *strokes* are the sense of acceptance, affirmation and inclusion which make group membership a positive experience; and *stimulation* is what makes it interesting. If these needs are not met, group members are unlikely to relate well to one another, and the group's *purpose* is unlikely to be achieved.

## The Comfort/Challenge Dynamic

Effective groups—that is to say, those which are fulfilling their purpose—tend to feel both safe and challenging. As this diagram (overleaf) shows, this is not always the case.

In practice, people will not stay in a group in which they feel uncomfortable, nor in a group in which they are bored. In our experience people will, consciously or not, prioritize comfort over challenge, which means that groups which see themselves primarily as support groups will often be more successful than groups which embrace the challenge of transformation.

But dare we ignore this challenge? If God's purpose is our transformation, it is vital that our groups have a strong discipleship agenda.

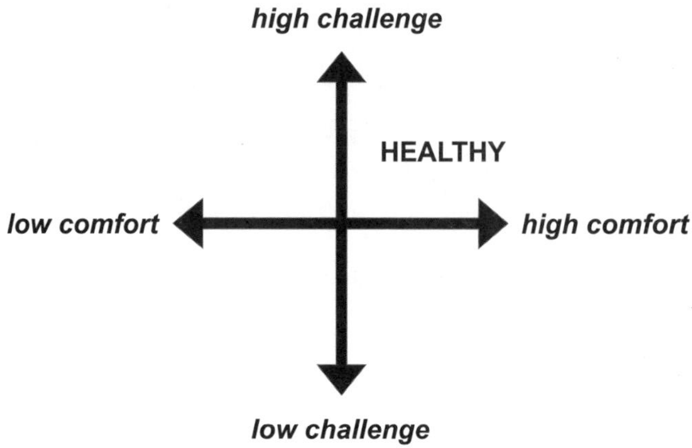


## Questions for Reflection

- How can you ensure that what goes on in your meetings is relevant to people's everyday lives?
- Taken alongside the Sunday gatherings in church and individuals' prayer times at home, what part does your small group play in growing disciples?
- In what ways might you choose to be accountable to one another in your group, and why?

# 3 How Does the Leadership of Your Group Facilitate its Purpose?

In this chapter, we focus on the role of the small group leader, discussing issues relating to power and empowerment, and helping you to reflect on what you are doing and why.

When it comes to small groups, there are actually a number of possible leadership roles, though in many cases these are held by the same person, which is not, we would suggest, something to aim for. Four common leadership roles in a small group are:

- *The leader(s)*—this is the person or people who are designated as having overall responsibility for the group.
- *The convenor(s)*—this is the person or people who might take on the administrative tasks for the group, for example, reminding people of a change of venue, or letting people know if the group is not meeting. This role is often held by the group leader.
- *The host(s)*—this is the person or people who are responsible for the physical (or virtual) space in which the group is meeting, which may also involve providing refreshments.
- *The facilitator(s)*—this is the person or people who are responsible for leading the meeting on a particular occasion. If the main purpose of the group is Bible study, then this may involve preparing questions for discussion around a particular biblical passage. If the main purpose of the group is prayer, then this may involve preparing some prompts for prayer or prayer activities. If the group has a time of worship as part of their meeting, it may involve preparing and leading this too.

Can you identify any other common leadership roles in a small group?

Which of these leadership roles do you see yourself as holding, regularly or occasionally?

We recognize that each of these leadership roles may be held by more than one person, which is often the case when married couples are involved in leading small groups. However, we would like to suggest that having as wide a range of people involved as possible is a good thing. In *Making Missional Disciples through Small Groups*, Singlehurst and Withers are keen to establish the importance of 'participation' and 'contribution' in small groups as well as in wider church life, and we firmly agree with them on this.[9] In what follows, we use the term 'leader' to include anyone who may take the facilitator role, as well as the person with overall responsibility for the group.

## Leadership and the Issue of Power

Any form of leadership role brings with it issues relating to power. You may not consider yourself to have significant power as a small group leader, but there are different forms of power, some more obvious than others. John Heron, in his work relating to group facilitation, suggests that group leaders often possess one (or more) of three types of power: tutelary, political or charismatic.[10] *Tutelary* power refers to the way the leader is seen as knowledgeable or experienced in a particular area, with the expectation that this knowledge and experience is to be shared with the group. So in the case of a Bible study group the leader would often be seen to be particularly knowledgeable about the Bible. *Political* power refers to the fact that the group leader may have the power to make decisions that affect the group, for example, what materials to use, or whether or not to meet over the summer. And finally, *charismatic* power refers to the influence that the leader has over other members of group simply through 'their way of being and behaving.'[11]

There are many different ways of understanding and evaluating what gives an individual power, but in a group context one of the key things that gives a leader power is the group itself. As Raths notes, 'Power comes from others'; it is 'interpersonal.'[12] Ultimately, if the group recognizes the leader as leader, that in itself gives them a certain degree of power and *vice versa:* if the group rejects the leadership of an individual, then their power is reduced or undermined. And if power does not rest with the leader, where does it lie? You might notice who speaks the most in meetings, and to whom other members do or do not defer.

So where does this brief discussion about the nature of power get us? Ultimately, a key question to consider is this:

> How—as leader—are you helping your small group achieve its purpose(s)?

In other words, how are you using your power as leader to empower other members of your group as they seek to live as faithful disciples of Jesus in the twenty-first century? No pressure!

We would suggest that a key role of the small group leader is to empower others. Timothy Keller suggests that a good group leader will 'correctly understand and handle the Bible passage,' but also '*encourage and train the people… to do this for themselves*. Don't fall into the trap of spoon-feeding people.'[13] A good group leader and, in particular, a good group *facilitator*, plays a vital role in supporting and enabling the other members of the group in their growth as disciples, and a key part of that is growing in confidence. As Singlehurst and Withers point out, 'Discipleship is enabled as application takes place within the supportive and accountable framework of the small group, and powerful transformation can occur as the group journeys together.'[14]

## Facilitating a Small Group

When it comes to facilitating a small group, the issue of tutelary power becomes particularly important. To what extent are you as facilitator—the person leading the discussion or study—seen as being especially knowledgeable? And to what extent are you expected to simply impart this knowledge?

In Anna's research, it was interesting to note how the role of 'expert' emerged in a number of the groups involved. For example, in one group, the person who seemed to be viewed as the expert of the group was regularly deferred to when people were unsure what a particular Bible passage or verse meant, and also to check that they understood things correctly. If they had the same answer as the resident expert, then it must be the right answer![15] However, this highlights one of the dangers of being viewed as an expert—your contributions can unintentionally shut down discussions and actually prevent fruitful explorations if people become too fixated on finding the 'right' answer.

We suggest that a major clue as to what your role entails is in the name: *facilitator.* This involves supporting a discussion that enables people to engage, explore and contribute, without feeling they need to have the right answers. So, as far as possible, avoid becoming the arbiter of correct answers, and instead seek to be 'one voice among many.'[16]

## The Comfort/Challenge Dynamic

A key factor in enabling challenge to have a positive role in groups is the leader or facilitator's approach; in fact John Heron considers confronting to be one of the dimensions of group facilitation, 'which is to do with how to raise consciousness about resistances to, and avoidances of, things that need to be faced and dealt with.'[17] This might include the systematic avoidance of silence in group meetings—or of the fact that the group is a collection of well-off individuals in a deprived area. So the comfort / challenge dynamic is relevant to the group process as well as to the content—and the group leader needs to be aware of the pressure to collude with the tendency to choose comfort and avoid challenge. Are you willing to challenge this choice when necessary, and to help group members learn to be comfortable with the uncomfortable?

This is complicated by the fact that, as we saw in the previous chapter, the individual needs of each group member for acceptance, affirmation and inclusion (strokes) must also be met in order to ensure their ongoing participation and commitment. The same applies to the needs of the group as a whole, which is why team-building exercises of all kinds are used in every imaginable context to ensure that group members relate well to one another and work effectively together towards the achievement of their task or purpose. It does not have to involve visiting an outdoor activity centre(!), but it is worth taking time to grow relationships in your group, whether through social events or specific team-building exercises.

We might reframe this relational dimension as a set of norms which most small group leaders would want to establish. How would you rate your group against these values, and how might you as group leader nurture them more effectively?

- Our group feels like a safe place (though not always a comfortable place) in which to ask questions, experiment and take risks; it is a 'Have a go' culture.
- We practise excellent listening and appropriate self-disclosure, honesty and vulnerability; we value openness, and are glad to welcome new members.
- Everyone participates, everyone is exploring and developing their gifts; it is a culture of growth in discipleship, recognizing 'every-member ministry' and 'the priesthood of all believers'.[18]
- We are comfortable talking about God and sharing our faith in everyday language, which makes it easier to use God-talk in everyday life.
- We expect to share our faith outside the group, and encourage and support one another in our relationships with those who are not yet Christians.[19]

The leader's role in establishing this kind of group culture might be summarized as three functions: guardian (of the group's purpose); guide; and gift-releaser.[20]

As the above list suggests, being a group leader involves balancing what might be called the vertical and the horizontal dimensions of group life. In other words, it is about going deeper with God *and* going deeper with one another. This will only be possible if group members are truly open both to God and to one another—open to giving and also open to receiving.

## Questions for Reflection

- How would you rate your group on the five criteria listed above? In each case, how does your leadership style help or hinder?
- Might there be another potential guard, guide or gift-releaser in your group? If so, how might you support their growth in this area?
- As leader, how do you discern whether the group needs more comfort or more challenge as you go on learning to live 'The Way'?

# 4 How Does Your Group's Context Help it Achieve its Purpose?

As we continue to explore the various factors which can help or hinder a group in achieving its purpose, the *context* in which it meets is likely to be significant. Key issues here are time and place—or history and geography.

Stand right back for a moment and imagine your group as the subject of a book or a film. How would you describe its setting, with reference both to its twenty-first century context and to its global location? What might be the implications of your description?

## Group Culture

Questions like this get us thinking about the *culture* in which we live and, as we dig deeper, the various layers of our subculture, including the national, local, social and ecclesial. This brings us back to the concept of norms, and the extent to which we accept or challenge the values of the culture we are part of. As Paul writes, 'Do not conform to the pattern of this world, but be transformed by the renewing of your mind' (Rom 12.2).

In reflecting on the culture of a group, Brené Brown has developed ten questions to highlight aspects of a group that can easily remain unacknowledged or overlooked. The ten questions are:[21]

- What behaviours are rewarded or punished?
- Where and how are people actually spending their resources (time, money, attention)?
- What rules and expectations are followed, enforced and ignored?
- Do people feel safe and supported talking about how they feel and asking for what they need?
- What are the sacred cows? Who is most likely to tip them? Who stands the cows back up?
- What stories are legend and what values do they convey?
- What happens when someone fails, disappoints, or makes a mistake?

- How is vulnerability (uncertainty, risk and emotional exposure) perceived?
- How prevalent are shame and blame and how are they showing up?
- What is the collective tolerance for discomfort? Is the discomfort of learning, trying new things, and giving and receiving feedback normalized, or is there a high premium put on comfort (and how does that look)?

The answers to these questions about the culture of the group constitute its *norms;* they may be in line with the purpose of the group, or they may potentially undermine it. If, when reflecting on these questions, there are aspects of your group's culture that you would like to change, then how might you go about it?

Another factor that might determine the culture of the group, and is also part of its context, is the length of time the group has been running. Many will be familiar with Bruce Tuckman's model of the five stages of a group—forming, storming, norming, performing and adjourning (or mourning);[22] there are various alternative models, such as John Heron's sequence of wintertime, springtime, summertime and autumn.[23] These models usefully highlight the fact that all groups go through stages, and what is appropriate for an established group may not be appropriate for a new group, and *vice versa.* Is your group in the forming or wintertime stage—where people may not yet feel comfortable with one another, and levels of trust and vulnerability are still relatively low? In the early stages of a group, it is important to ensure that people feel comfortable, rather than challenged, whereas greater challenge will be a good thing later on.

## Small Changes—Big Difference?

You may think that you cannot change the context of your group, and this is true when you are thinking big—you cannot relocate yo[illegible]s historically or geographically. But when you think small, you [illegible]hat some of the things you take for granted are in fact negotiable. [illegible]e group could decide to meet at a different time, or at a different venue or v[illegible]ues. This might be a permanent change or it might not: when a young couple have a baby, meeting in their home may allow both parents to continue to join in. Or you could occasionally meet online and earlier in the day, so that the couple spending the northern winter in Australia can participate! Simply trying something like this can generate lots of material for experiential learning, as you reflect on how the group works differently in a new context. But if this is a shocking idea, it suggests that you have embraced 'Thou shalt not experiment' as one of your unwritten rules, thereby denying yourself and the group a significant experience to learn from in terms of what might help or hinder the effective functioning of the group.

Thinking small, there are many things you could change. *Time-wise,* would a different time of day or day of the week work better? Or a different frequency? If disciple-making for the real world is your core purpose, then meeting online over a weekday lunchtime might help you keep the focus on the context in which people spend most of their waking hours, especially if they work in an office, or from home, or caring for dependants.

And what about meeting in a different *place?* This could be as radical as meeting online or as easy as moving from the living room to the kitchen or dining area. In our experience, this simple change of furniture can make a big difference: the sofas and armchairs around the fire may be wonderfully relaxing, but they are likely to promote comfort rather than challenge, enhancing passive receptivity (and nodding off!) rather than active engagement. Sitting upright around a kitchen or dining table, on the other hand, makes it much easier to involve the group in activities such as comparing texts, writing or responding with creative materials. So if the group begins with a meal around a table, it is worth clearing everything away afterwards and staying at the table—perhaps encouraging people to change places.

**What about meeting in a different place?**

If you always meet in the same place, there will be much that is taken for granted, including some important issues around power and control. Meeting in the leader's home, for example, means that the leader is the host(ess) and the others are guests, with all the social implications and expectations associated with both roles: the host probably decides what refreshments are offered and when, how the furniture is organized and so on; the guests are expected to arrive at an appropriate time, and resist commenting on the mess! Meeting in the homes of various members will redress the balance somewhat, and will mean that each person who hosts will, deliberately or not, reveal more about themselves and their lives than those who are not able to host, or choose not to. What people reveal in online groups is a fascinating issue, offering one another little glimpses of their usually private worlds.

Meeting in a relatively neutral place, such as a church room, or a café or pub, will have a different dynamic: who is perceived as owning the space, and thus being the host (even if not physically present)? To what extent can group members feel at home there, enjoying enough of a sense of shared ownership to feel comfortable? A relatively public meeting place will also make the group more accessible to non-members, but may also mean people feel less safe in terms of being vulnerable.

Meeting outdoors is unusual in most climates, but definitely worth experimenting with; people might connect with God and with each other in very different ways, and it might feel closer to the real world. The fact that it feels different is partly to do with the physical environment, experienced through your five senses: the sights and sounds and smells (and tastes?) are different; it may be warmer or cooler than usual, and perhaps you can feel the sun or the wind on your skin. If the group is up for it, how about going away somewhere for a retreat day together? A rural location or a place with a garden would be ideal.

This brings us on to another significant issue: *the feel of the group.* How might you describe its atmosphere? Might others perceive it differently? What are the key factors at work here? It is worth reflecting on the interplay of the comfort/challenge dynamic, the group norms, issues of power and the role of the leader (as discussed in the previous chapter).

## Meeting Online

When the group meets *online,* that is, sharing time but not place, the feel of the group becomes even more significant. Each person exists in two places simultaneously—the (virtual) group space and their own personal space. If each person chooses which of these to pay attention to at any given moment, which do I choose and why? It will depend on a subconscious cost/benefit analysis of the two environments—for example, I might think, 'This discussion is getting boring…I'll just have a peep at my emails,' only to be brought back to the group with a jolt when I hear someone asking me a question! If the group feels good, and what goes on in the group meets my needs, I will opt in; if it does not, I will opt out—or choose to leave the meeting altogether, which would be much more difficult in a face-to-face group. This 'vote with your fingers' option illustrates how members of online groups are in some ways more powerful in this context, and perhaps more motivated by self-interest: it is easy to opt out altogether if I am tired, sending a quick apologies message to the leader at the last minute rather than choosing to turn up for the sake of the group as a whole.

Reflecting on our experience of online groups for church members, we identified various potential advantages and disadvantages:

### Possible Advantages of Meeting Online

- Good for people who live alone, are housebound or disabled, or do not like going out in the dark

- Good for parents of young children or those caring for dependants.
- Good for people who travel a lot.
- People can make themselves physically comfortable.
- People might feel safer, especially when sharing personal material, thus promoting self-disclosure.
- It is easier for enquirers to visit the group, and everyone's names are visible.
- People will generally be at home, in the everyday world where they live out their faith.
- The screenshare facility means that everyone can see the same text, image or video.
- The chat facility means that people can contribute information, raise questions, paste links, upload documents and so on.
- There is no need to provide (and possible pay for) a venue—or refreshments!

### Possible Disadvantages of Meeting Online

- People might lack broadband, or the necessary bandwidth for video-conferencing.
- People might not feel competent or confident using the online platform.
- Conversely, people who have been looking at a screen all day, perhaps in online meetings, might be 'Zoomed out'.
- People who share a home with others might have to deal with more distractions and interruptions.
- Privacy might be an issue for those who share a home—others might overhear what they are sharing, and (without headphones) other group members may be overheard.
- The physical separation may prevent a genuine sense of belonging together, partly because the informal face-to-face interactions cannot happen,
- People might revert to audience mode, watching and listening but not participating.
- It is difficult to provide physical resources, and people might lack the facility to print material in advance.

Looking at the above lists, different factors will be relevant to different groups. But there are some general principles and practices which can enhance the effectiveness of online groups for disciple-making, the most basic of which is the need to maximize interaction; the risk of passivity is greater online, so the leader will need to work harder to keep everyone engaged. This can be quite a challenge, partly because the online context tends to have a levelling effect, reducing the power of the leader. Simply inviting people to sit at their desk or the kitchen table means they can easily participate in writing or creative activities, and the use of Zoom rooms (without other groups eavesdropping) can be very effective, with an opportunity to report back to the whole group if appropriate.

Constant interaction online can be very tiring, and there are advantages to facilitating some more solitary activities. This could include leading a reflection or meditation, or asking people to read or write something. (See the next chapter for more about online content.)

## Questions for Reflection

- Does the time and day when your group meets help it to achieve its purpose? What difference might a change make?
- How might meeting in a different room or a different venue affect the feel of the group and its effectiveness?
- Your group may have met online for a time, or may still do so. What have you learnt about making the group work in this context?
- In terms of disciple-making, what might be some advantages of meeting online?

# 5 How are Materials Used to Achieve Your Group's Purposes?

'Small groups are a means to an end, not an end in themselves.' Although you might agree with this quite readily—and it is a basic premise of this booklet—it does bring us back to the key issue of *purpose,* and how you can ensure that your group keeps moving towards its fulfilment. In earlier chapters we have reflected on the need to clarify the group's purpose, and on the significance of leadership and context in achieving that purpose; here we focus on the *materials* and *methods* used.

> What materials and methods do you currently use in your small group to aid your discussions and reflections?

The fact that small groups are sometimes called Bible study groups raises an interesting question: does this mean that the group's purpose or end is to study the Bible? It may simply be shorthand for a deep commitment to 'doing' the Word (Jas 1.22), but to an outsider the name would probably imply studying the Bible for its own sake. There is nothing wrong with this if the group's explicit purpose is to help members develop their knowledge and understanding of the Bible (as they might study the works of Shakespeare), in which case the materials and methods used will facilitate intellectual engagement—as in traditional academic education.

Small groups may also be referred to as house groups or home groups (a flat is as good as a house), or midweek groups, which does distinguish them from what happens in church on Sundays but does not reveal much about their purpose. However, calling them life groups or discipleship groups makes their purpose more explicit: here group / church members 'work out their salvation' in everyday life, trusting that God is at work in them, transforming them 'to will and to act according to his good purpose' (Phil 2.12–13). Paul's exhortation begins 'Therefore…' linking it directly with the famous 'Song of Christ's Humility' (Phil 2.5–11) which precedes it. In other words, if the purpose of your group is to help people grow into the likeness of Christ, you will need to spend time engaging together with the Scriptures which reveal him to us—studying the Bible, in fact.[24] But this is a more holistic focus, and the materials and methods used will need to facilitate spiritual, emotional, social and practical engagement, not just intellectual: it is about heart as much as head.

## Four Ws—or Five?

It is hard to imagine even the most intellectual Bible study group spending its entire time studying the Bible: our experience of life outside the church suggests that most group meetings begin with some kind of introduction and end with some kind of action plan or commitment to follow up. One way of formalizing this sequence for Christian groups is to use the 4Ws introduced by Phil Potter: the idea is that the meeting begins with *welcome*, followed by *worship*, before focusing on the *word* and its application: *works* or *witness*.[25] Some add another W for the *wind* of the Holy Spirit, who brings it all to life.

The head / heart distinction is worth bearing in mind when making decisions about materials and methods for each of the Ws, so that the whole meeting feels balanced. As far as the comfort / challenge balance goes, the *welcome* needs to promote comfort, though a degree of challenge may be helpful in setting the scene for the word section.

These two dimensions are also relevant to decisions about *worship*, but our focus here is on materials and methods for the word and works components, given that few groups would see welcome and / or worship as their primary purpose. There are plenty of practical suggestions for all the Ws on the Cell-Ideas website and in print, and many ideas and resources for creative worship in congregations can be adapted for small groups.[26]

Because we are assuming that the purpose of most groups is related to members' individual and corporate transformation into the likeness of Christ, characterized by his love for the world, we are prioritizing the *word* which reveals him and the *works* he inspires. So what are the options when choosing material and methods for engaging with Scripture and responding in practice? As well as considering the head / heart and comfort / challenge dimensions, there are other factors which will affect your choices, a major one being whether the group is expected to follow a curriculum decided by the church leadership. This may mean staying with the focus of the previous Sunday's sermon, perhaps with specially-prepared materials, or using a resource to develop people's discipleship in a particular way—for example, the Prayer Course[27] or the Bible Course, both widely used.[28]

If each group is free to choose its own material, resources such as these may be a useful option, though both involve watching a video together, either online or downloaded. This and other practical considerations, such as cost, will come into play, as will the amount of preparation needed: do members of your group expect to spend time on pre-work (as in a book group), or is it only the person facilitating who needs to prepare? This immediately brings us back to norms and the group's written or unwritten rules about materials and methods, such as:

- We are not keen on the Old Testament
- We approve of N T Wright
- We like Lectio Divina
- We do not like Ignatian meditation
- We prefer whole-group discussion to mini-groups
- Some of us love arty things and some of us do not!

If you are the leader of the group, are you prepared to highlight or question any of these norms? Might there be a time to reduce the comfort a little and allow more challenge, as people learn to be comfortable being uncomfortable?

## Content and Process

Considering *materials* in more detail, we see two aspects of *content* in a typical word / works session. First comes the raw material itself: often a Bible passage, though it might be something else, like a picture, a video or a poem. Then there are all the tools you use to engage with the material, for example, commentaries and concordances for group members to consult about the Bible passage, or some diagrams to explain christological heresies, or photos someone took in the Holy Land to illustrate a gospel story about the Sea of Galilee. In the case of a Bible passage, the possible tools are almost endless—just search online for 'group Bible study resources,' many of which are free.[29]

It is worth bearing in mind that whatever tools you choose to help facilitate your engagement with the Bible are likely to have an influence on the kind of discussion that follows. There are no neutral materials—every writer is writing from a particular perspective and a particular theological standpoint. So if the questions posed by the materials are very head-based, then you are more likely to have a discussion that focuses on the more intellectual or academic aspects of the passage (such as authorship or who the original hearers were). If you select materials that are very heart-based, then you are more likely to have a discussion that focuses on the emotional or personal aspects of the passage (how does this verse make you feel? or what does this teach you about yourself?). We suggest that the ideal would be a good balance between the two, so you may need to adapt the materials you are using to achieve this. As Anna's research indicated, the best discussions emerged when the group leaders had taken materials and adapted them specifically for their group, bringing together the expertise found in the study materials with their own expertise about the group to enable really fruitful and engaging discussions.[30]

There are plenty of other tried-and-tested practices which cost nothing and require minimal preparation; Lectio Divina and the imaginative meditation approach associated with Ignatius Loyola have both been practised for hundreds of years. Many have become familiar with 'Dwelling in the Word' or the 'wondering' questions of Godly Play; all of these lend themselves to a creative response, such as drawing, writing or collage, from which the Works application flows. And an inductive method such as Discovery Bible Study has the works component built into its wide-ranging questions.[31] At the end of a Bible study, perhaps as you turn to prayer, you might simply ask, 'What did you find most comforting?' and 'What did you find most challenging?'

**'What did you find most comforting?' and 'What did you find most challenging?'**

We also see three main categories of *method* or process, depending on how the group is configured. First, the whole group will probably stay together for the beginning of the word section (as well as for the welcome and most of the worship), so everyone starts on the same page with the Bible and / or other material. This allows for input, discussion and brief sharing, and will maximize comfort for some, especially if they favour a head approach. Secondly, the group might divide into smaller groups or pairs, allowing for a much higher contribution level, and perhaps helping the quieter members. These mini-groups may enable people to cope with a greater degree of challenge, especially at the heart end of the spectrum, so they risk sharing more deeply. Thirdly, group members may be invited to spend time quietly alone, without necessarily moving, as they engage with a particular head or heart activity, and as they consider the works they are being called to as they apply the word. In any one meeting, group members may experience all of these configurations, probably finishing all together as people share their works commitments or other takeaways. It is important to allow time for this works section, as it can easily get squeezed out.

Needless to say, all these options for materials and methods can be combined in more and more ways as you reflect on and learn from your experiences.

## What Works Online?

One option we have not considered here is the *online* option, despite listing so many advantages in the previous chapter. It is interesting to look back over the above discussion of materials and methods with an online group in mind, noticing which options might work in your context. For example, the screenshare facility means that it is easy for everyone to look at the same text or image, perhaps using PowerPoint, and an online whiteboard is good for brainstorms and other kinds of list-making. Breakout groups or Zoom rooms allow more intimate discussion and sharing, without hearing or being overheard by other groups. And the fact that people can mute their microphone enables confident singing or liturgical responses and, with their video camera off as well, they may enjoy trying new experiments in prayer.

## Questions for Reflection

- Thinking back on the materials you have been using most recently, to what extent do they enable both head and heart-based engagement?
- Do the methods and materials that you currently use allow for a healthy balance of both comfort and challenge?
- What new methods or materials might you like to experiment with?
- How would a potential new member or an enquirer find your group? What might they struggle with?
- How relevant is your content to people's ordinary everyday lives?

# 6 Conclusion

In this final chapter, we suggest some tools for ongoing reflection and evaluation, as well as offering some thoughts on what to do when small groups go wrong.

In chapter three we offered a set of norms or values which could be used as the basis for a discussion about the health of the group, and in chapter four we highlighted Brené Brown's questions about group culture, especially those aspects that may go unnoticed. If your group has been running for some time, it might be especially helpful to reflect on these questions and ask yourself whether there are any areas of the group's life that need to be addressed.

In relation to the culture of the group, another resource is the Blob Tree. Originally developed by behavioural psychologist Pip Wilson, it can be a useful tool in helping people reflect on how they see themselves in a given setting.[32] You might share a Blob Tree image with your group occasionally, and ask the members which blob they feel they relate to, and why. This may provide a useful way of bringing to the surface some of the group's interpersonal dynamics, and if necessary, gently exploring and perhaps challenging these. Various versions of the Blob Tree can be found online and downloaded free of charge.

We also briefly referred to the different stages of a group's life and identified some models of what might be expected at each stage of a group's development. There is plenty of material online about recognizing the stages of Tuckman's model and helping the group to make progress from one to the next.

As part of Anna's research, she made use of a questionnaire that asked members of small groups the following question: 'As a result of being in this group, have you been influenced to do any of the following?' A range of options was then offered, each linked to one of the Five Marks of Mission.[33] For example, 'Made changes to your lifestyle choices in order to limit your impact on the environment' was listed as one of the options, linking with the fifth Mark of Mission ('To strive to safeguard the integrity of creation and sustain and renew the life of the earth').[34] You might find it helpful to create opportunities for your group to reflect, both as individuals and together, on what contribution your small group is making to your personal discipleship, as well as on its wider impact. Is it helping you to live more Jesus-shaped lives, both individually and collectively?

## When Small Groups Go Wrong...

By going wrong we mean that some aspect of the group is causing problems for the group as a whole. Examples of this might include a breakdown of the relationship between two or more members of the group, an issue with the group culture, or a failure of leadership, to name a few common problems. The tools that we have suggested above, along with other means of reflecting upon and evaluating the group, may help you diagnose the problem. If a group has gone badly wrong, the group will no longer be functioning as it was hoped it would and could. It will no longer be helping people to live more Jesus-shaped lives, nor equipping its members for everyday discipleship.

### So What Can You Do?

Ultimately, it depends on what has gone wrong. For example, if the issue is a breakdown of relationships between two or members of the group, then clearly the ideal solution is reconciliation, so that healing can take place, both for the specific individuals as well as for the group as a whole. If this is not possible, it may be necessary for a mix-up to take place, so that a number of small groups might choose to disband and then reform with a different mix of people—though this will not be possible in every context.

If the issue is that an unhealthy and unhelpful group culture has developed, leading to group habits and norms that are preventing people from growing in their discipleship, then these need to be addressed. As noted already, the tools we have highlighted might help you diagnose the issue and then, as a group, you will need to explore how best to move forwards.

If the issue is that you feel you can no longer lead the group, for example, if you do not feel your leadership is accepted or valued, or if you have been directly challenged about your leadership, then this can be hugely painful as well as difficult to navigate. We would suggest that you talk to someone you trust and seek their advice, and also speak to your church leader about the issues.

One further problem is that the group appears to stagnate. This might be a sign that the group has reached the autumn phase, to use John Heron's model, and it might be time for the group to end, or 'adjourn,' as Bruce Tuckman would say. This does not necessarily mean it has gone wrong, though it can feel like this; it may simply have reached a stage where it is no longer able to fulfil the purpose for which it was originally formed. This can be painful but, as Heron notes, it can also be an opportunity for people to 'give thanks and go their way.'[35] At this point it will be helpful to give the group space to share what they have valued about the group and to mark its ending in an appropriate way.

Perhaps the biggest question for any small group is about its effectiveness in growing disciples—people who are continually growing closer to Jesus and learning to live increasingly Jesus-shaped lives. Jesus himself taught that those who came to him thirsty and trusted him to fill them would in turn overflow with life for others:

> On the last and greatest day of the festival, Jesus stood and said in a loud voice, 'Let anyone who is thirsty come to me and drink. Whoever believes in me, as Scripture has said, rivers of living water will flow from within him.' By this he meant the Spirit, whom those who believed in him were later to receive… (John 7.37–39)

It is our hope that in your small groups, people will be able to come together to be refreshed and sustained, so that rivers of living water will flow from within them as they go back into the world to live ever more Jesus-shaped lives.

## Notes

1 A Creedon, *Do Small Groups Work? Biblical Engagement and Transformation* (London: SCM Press, 2021).

2 L Singlehurst and T Withers, *Making Missional Disciples through Small Groups: Why Small Groups are Essential for Today* (Grove Mission and Evangelism booklet MEv136).

3 T Douglas, *Groups: Understanding People Gathered Together* (London: Tavistock, 1983).

4 A Creedon, *Do Small Groups Work?, op cit*, p 160.

5 A Creedon, *Do Small Groups Work?, op cit*, p 160.

6 W Wink, *Transforming Bible Study* (London: SCM Press, 2nd edition, 1981) p 82.

7 J Adair, *Action-Centred Leadership* (Aldershot: Gower Publishing Co, 1979).

8 E Berne, *Games People Play* (New York: Grove Press, 1964).

9 L Singlehurst and T Withers, *Making Missional Disciples, op cit*, p 4.

10 J Heron, *The Complete Facilitator's Handbook* (London: Kogan Page, 1999) p 19.

11 *ibid* p 20.

12 L Raths, 'Power in Small Groups,' *The Journal of Educational Sociology, Vol 28, No 3*, 1954, pp 97-103 (p 97).

13 T Keller, *Galatians: Gospel Matters* (Epsom: Good Book Company, 2013) p 50 (emphasis added).

14 L Singlehurst and T Withers, *Making Missional Disciples, op cit*, p 25.

15 A Creedon, *Do Small Groups Work? op cit*, p 97.

16 L J Lawrence, *The Word in Place: Reading the New Testament in Contemporary Contexts* (London: SPCK, 2009) p 105.

17 J Heron, *The Complete Facilitator's Handbook, op cit*, p 179.

18 Singlehurst and Withers comment that, 'As we embrace the value of everyone involved, our small group gives us the perfect place in a safe environment for our faith to grow from passive to active.' *Making Missional Disciples, op cit*, p 16.

19 For Singlehurst and Withers, the primary purpose of small groups is to enable evangelism. So 'The role of a small group is to spend a few moments each week praying for the relationships we have, praying for one another to keep reaching out.' *Making Missional Disciples, op cit*, p 17.

20 A Taylor and R Wilson, *Small Groups, Big Mission* (Loughborough: Fusion UK, 2018) pp 76–77.

21 B Brown, *Daring Greatly: How the Courage to be Vulnerable Transforms the Way We Live, Love, Parent, and Lead* (London: Penguin Books, 2012) pp 174–175.

22 B W Tuckman and M A C Jensen, 'Stages of Small-Group Development Revisited,' *Group and Organization Studies*, Vol *2, No 4, 1977,* pp 419–427.

23 J Heron, *The Complete Facilitator's Handbook, op cit*, pp 51–52.

24 Compare Romans 8.29: 'For those God foreknew he also predestined to be conformed to the image of his Son, that he might be the firstborn among many brothers and sisters.'

25 P Potter, *The Challenge of Cell Church: Getting to Grips with Cell Church Values* (Abingdon: BRF, 2001); Singlehurst and Withers, *Making Missional Disciples, op cit.*

26 http://www.cell-ideas.co.uk

27 https://prayercourse.org

28 https://www.biblesociety.org.uk/explore-the-bible/the-bible-course/

29 For example, Lyfe material from https://www.biblesociety.org.uk/explore-the-bible/lyfe/ or material on many topics from https://homegroups.org.uk

30 A Creedon, *Do Small Groups Work? op cit, p 156.*

31 https://discoverapp.org/discovery-bible-study

32 P Wilson and I Long, *The Big Book of Blob Trees* (Abingdon: Routledge, 2009).

33 A Creedon, *Do Small Groups Work?, op cit*, p 176.

34 Anglican Consultative Council, *Mission in a Broken World: Report of ACC-8: Wales 1990* (London: Church House Publishing, 1990) p 101.

35 J Heron, *The Complete Facilitator's Handbook, op cit*, 52.